Marina Branch

DISCARD

Marina Branch   270030

j394 Belting, Natalia Maree
B   Winter's eve.   Holt, 1969

SAN MATEO PUBLIC LIBRARY
SAN MATEO, CALIF.

1. Holidays- Gt. Brit. 2. Fasts
and feasts I. Title

7/70   459

WINTER'S EVE

Books for Young People by Natalia Belting

Winter's Eve
Christmas Folk
The Stars Are Silver Reindeer
The Earth Is on a Fish's Back
Calendar Moon
The Sun Is a Golden Earring
Elves and Ellefolk: Tales of Little People
Indy and Mr. Lincoln
Verity Mullens and the Indian
Cat Tales

NATALIA BELTING

WINTER'S EVE

illustrated by Alan E. Cober

HOLT, RINEHART AND WINSTON
New York   Chicago   San Francisco

Text Copyright © 1969 by Natalia Belting.
Illustrations Copyright © 1969 by Alan E. Cober.
All rights reserved, including the right to reproduce
this book or portions thereof in any form.
Published simultaneously in Canada by Holt, Rinehart
and Winston of Canada, Limited.
SBN: 03-082931-3 (Trade)
SBN: 03-087932-1 (HLE)
Library of Congress Catalog Card Number: 73-85425
Printed in the United States of America
First Edition
Design by Hilda Scott

WINTER'S EVE

Autumn stains
Hedge and hill
Russet,
Spreads red
Lambent
Down the ghylls,
Burnishes the languid streams.

Chill creeps
Out of the north,
The north-east;

Rimes the gossamer
Where it hangs
Over the furze
And teazle,
Dripping dry,
The pixies' tatters and rags;

Frosts holly berries,
The green buckler ferns
By the ponds
Where the moorhens come,
Far back in the woods.

The swallows
Gather on ridge tiles
And chimney caps;
Finches glean
The barley stubble;
Jays chuckle
In the gray birch thicket

In cart ways and lanes
The fading sun
Yellows clouds—
Drifting
Like dust—
Of fairies flitting,

For now
Is the time
The spirits go abroad,

Now comes the time of evil,
The dark time of the year,
Winter's Eve.

September 28

Michaelmas Eve
And the days before,
   Carrots are cropped,
   Crab apples picked,
   Turnips turned up
      By the girls,
       Small lasses, great,
   Picked where the birds sowed,
   Cropped where the winds
      Sowed wild,
        In the plow land,
      Sowed wanton
        In hedge row,
        Meadow,
        And yard land.

The girls,
No matter their age,
   When they strew them to dry,
   On the barn floor,

>   Trace letters
>   Of carrots and apples
>   And turnips,
>
>   Trace the names
>   Of the boys
>   They've a mind to wed.

The boys range the hills,
Coppice and thicket,
> Nutting;
> Stuff hats full,
> Shirts full,
> Sacks full,

For Crack-a-Nut Night,
> The Eve of St. Michael's
> Michaelmas Eve.

The Eve of St. Michael's
The struan bakes
  On the griddle
  Before the fire,
      The Michaelmas bannock
      Made of new grain,
          Three-sided,
          Nine-sided.
The struan is spread
On this side,
That,
With buttermilk, flour and eggs
All the night through,
      So it grows
      As it bakes.

(Before it is done,
The cook takes a bit,
Rolls it up in a ball,
Casts it over her shoulder,
Says,
  "Here you are,
  Devil, demon, sprite.
  Now stay away
  From me and mine
  Til another St. Michael's Day.")

Then baked,
The struan is broke
 And shared
  With the fire, that gobbles its bite,
  With the poor,
  And the neighbors,
   Whoever
   Comes in at the door
   St. Michael's Day.

September 29

In the gray, wet
Cook fire smoke and mist
  At Michaelmas dawn,
      All the townsfolk go out,
      Save the lame and the old,
      And the newborn,

      Circuit the graveyard;
      Three times
      Walk sunwise
      Round the wattled close;

      Then exchange
      As they go home,
      Bunches of carrots,
      Scrubbed clean,
      Tight-tied
      With scarlet thread,
      To prosper the year.

Michaelmas morning
  The boys and the men
  Gang after a leader,
    Gang where he goes,
    Gang the streets and the lanes,
      Pudding-pye hill,
      The fairy mound,

      The Devil's rock,
      Brimstone Topping.

  Gang over the pickets
  And over the stiles,
      Over grave stones,
      Druid-circle stones,

      Needle stones,
      Eye stones;
  Clamber, pitch
  The length of the rockfall,
  The course of the waterfall.

The leader goes
Where no leader
Has gone,

Goes,
Til ganging behind
Only one comes,
      The leader,
      Next St. Michael's Day.

St. George comes to town,
St. George and the Dragon,
  Hobby the Horse,
  Old Betsey, the Doctor,
  The Letter-In,
     All guised for their parts
     This Michaelmas Day;

Parade through the town,
Dance with the townsfolk,
  Dance
  The Michaelmas dances:
     The Fighting Cocks,
     The Waddling Ducks,

     The reel of Tulloch,
     The dance of the Swords.

Then everyone shares
In the Michaelmas feast:

Roast goose,
Turnips and pork,
Mutton and dumplings,
Wild plum pudding,
          Struan cake.

(*After September 29*)

When the moon comes new
Past Michaelmas,
   The girls make a curtsey,
   The boys make a bow,
      Say, "Bless me, moon,
      I bless you."

And those who sleep
That new moon night,
   Heads pillowed on turf,
     (Sliced in three slices,
        That selfsame night,)

Dream
What will pass
   Til again, at Michaelmas,
   The moon is new.

(*After September 29*)

One of the weeks
At Winter's Eve
The Goose Fair is held.

The fat stubble geese
Are herded to town,
   Cackling, flapping,
   Through Goose Gate,
   Down Goose Lane;

   They chase the dogs, yapping,
   Drive the pigs, squealing,
      Out of their way,

Raise clouds of dust,
Stamping around,

   Until they are sold,
   For their meat,
   For their fat,
      To cure
      Winter sore throat,
      And cold on the lungs;

For their feathers,
> To fill
> New pillows,
> And make new beds;

For their quills,
> To make
> Pens for writing,
> And dulcimer plucks;

For guards,
> To guard
> Whatever needs guarding:
> Byre, or house or fold,
> Piglets, new lambs,
> Calves in the field.

October 6

St. Faith's Day
All young girls,
    Three by three,
    Bake a wedding cake.

    One by one
    Each one stirs.

    One by one
    Each one turns
        The cake as it bakes
        In the footed oven,
        In the hot coals,
Until they have turned it
Nine times.

Then the girls cut it
Into three pieces,
    Each piece into nine pieces more;
    Slip each piece
        Through the wedding ring
        Of a friend
        Married
        Seven years or more.

And when that is done
Each girl eats
    Her nine pieces of wedding cake,
    Goes to bed,
    Says,
"O good St. Faith, be kind tonight
And bring to me my heart's delight.
Let me my future husband view,
And be my vision chaste and true."

(*Anytime*)

At the ford
These evil nights
   The Washing Women,
   Hags,
   Wash the shrouds
   Of all who soon will die.

And the kelpie waits,
And the water bull,
   To drown
   The unwary traveler
   Who chances to come.

October 18

St. Luke's Day
Cattle, witched,
Are loosed of spells
If they be drove
Around a pollard ash,

   And infants freed
   From witches' curse
   And whooping cough
      When handed nine times
      Round an ash-wood bough.

(Around October 18, for a few days)

St. Luke's summer
Sunbeams ride the leaves
Of the rowan, gold,
On gold steeds,
   Set the beech-wood
   Smoldering red,

   Kindle green fire
   Deep in the damp
   Hazel-wood.

Shallops skim
Crystal red and purple streams
Of melted rainbows
Down-river from the hills,
   While pigs
    Gorge on mast
    In the oak-wood,

    Against the winter's
    Cold and dearth.

(*Anytime*)

At sky-set
Winter's Eve,
Unlucky folk
   See the black sow running,
    Know they will not
    Live the winter out.

Lucky folk
Whose right hands
Saucer
   Turf-fire ash,

See naught
Save autumn dark
Sweeping down.

October 25

St. Crispin's Day
The cobblers go out,
   Shoemakers,
   Prentices,
They all go out,
All the guildsmen,
The craftsmen,
   Go out,
       Rigged as gentlemen,
       Esquires and knights,

       Bishops, archbishops,
       Chancellors, clerks,
To honor St. Crispin,
The shoemaker's saint.

The townsmen turn out,
Country folk too,

To see the procession,
To see the good saint
    Riding ahead
    In spangles and fur,
    White satin breeches,
    White silk hose,
    Silver buckles on his shoes,
    Gold buttons on his coat,
    Crown on his head,
    And a crimson train
    Held off the ground
    By six small pages
    That follow his horse.

At the end of the day
The saint holds court,
  (As he did when alive,
  When king,
  Before he was saint),

Then dines
On sumptuous fare
  With the shoemaker's guild
  (The other guilds, too).

October 31

The witches
Ride out
On broomsticks
Warped thrice with the wind,
   Moon tassels
    Fixed to the reins,

Cloaked in skins
Of the shelly cow
(Half cow and half fish).

      Black gainst the stars
      The witches ride
      Screaming,
      Hallowmass eve.

Fires blaze
All Hallow e'en,
   Blaze gainst the witches,
   Hold them off,
   Stay their gathering together,
   Stay their mischief.
      Wood fires,
         In the scree
         Of the crags
         And the rock ledges;

      Dried-fern fires
         Caught on pitchforks,
         Set in the ground
         Round house and barn;

Candle fires,
    In turnips,
    Mangel-wurzels,
    Hollowed out and slashed.

Fires blaze
White hot; the coals
  Sain gainst evil
  Who walks
      Three times through them,
      Nine times round them,
  Sain gainst elf shot,
  Fairy blast,
  Fevers, boils and scab,

  Sain
Beast or man.

Haly on a cabbage stock and haly on a bean
Haly on a cabbage stock, this night's Hallow e'en.

Hallow e'en
The spirits are free.

Use the right charms
Use the right spells.

Hallow e'en,
If you must know
What's to come,
Ask the demons, they know.

Duck for apples,
Spin the plate;

Walk nine times
About a haycock,
Backwards, eyes shut.

Drop melted lead
In a dish of cold water,
Or the white of an egg
In a water glass full.

Watch in the graveyard,
See who's to die
Walk past you dumbly
Into a grave.

Stand in a plowed field
All by yourself
At midnight.
   If you hear
      Music for dancing,
      Fiddles and fifes,

   You can be sure
   You'll soon be wed.

   If you hear sobs
   And low, doleful cries,

   You can be sure
   When the furrows show green,
   You'll be dead.

The groliks go out,
    Young men and boys,
    Their faces
    Blacked with peat,
    Or hid
    By their long hair,
    Or masks.

They rush through the town,
Shrieking.
    Pelt houses with turnips,
    Unhinge gates,
    Overturn ricks,
    Strew dried peas
        The aisle of the church,

Loose horses stabled,
Drive them out,
Neighing,

Steal all the cabbages
Use them for footballs,
    Scatter and bruise them.

On Hallowmass eve
The groliks go out,
  And some are not seen,
  Ever again:

      They are seized by the spriggans,
        —The ghosts of the giants—
      Or the bogans,
      Or the demons,
           Or witches.

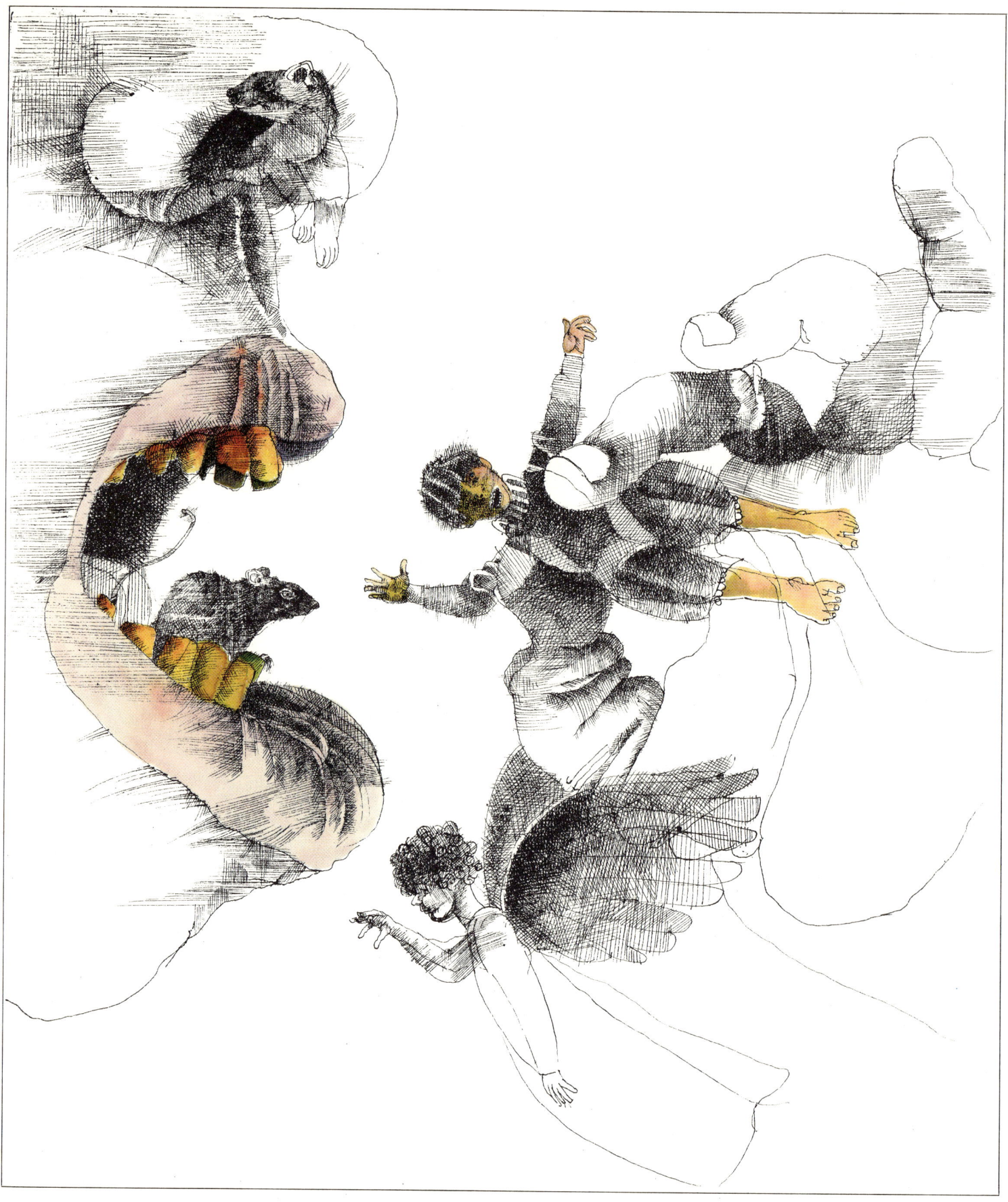

Demons, devils,
Trowes and spriggans,
Boggles, witches;

The evil host,
Those damned,
  The ghosts,
      Haunt the dark
      Winter's Eve,

      Haunt til daybreak
      Hallowmass,
            The first day
            Of winter.

Unless you say:
"St. Francis and St. Benedict,
Bless this house from wicked wight;
From the Night-mare and the goblin
That is hight Good-Fellow Robin;
Keep it from all evil spirits,
Fairies, weasels, rats and ferrets. . . ."

ABOUT THE AUTHOR: Assistant professor of history at the University of Illinois, Natalia Belting is a well-known author to our Holt list, with eight successful books to her credit. Miss Belting graduated from the University of Illinois, from which she also received her Masters and Ph.D. degrees. Her interest in historical research has given her the background information for each of her folklore interpretations. Along with her teaching and writing, Miss Belting finds time for her various hobbies, which include gardening, cooking, and excavating ancient artifacts of the Illinois Indians from her own property in Urbana, Illinois.

ABOUT THE ARTIST: Alan Cober, discouraged by an artist uncle, nearly became a lawyer instead of an artist. But luckily he didn't, and after his studies at the University of Vermont, he went on to the School of Visual Arts and the Pratt Graphic Center. He was chosen 1965 Artist of the Year by the Artists Guild of New York and was winner of the Gold Medal and the Hamilton King award given by the Society of Illustrators in 1968. Mr. Cober's distinctive graphic style has been seen on the pages of many popular magazines as well as in several children's books. The Cobers and their young son and daughter live in Ossining, New York.

ABOUT THE BOOK: With a pen-and-ink line technique, Mr. Cober brings a tremendous range to his illustrations from rich, full depth and luminosity to delicately beautiful accents, highlighted with full color. All blend well with Goudy Oldstyle text typeface and Michelangelo display typeface. The illustrations are reproduced by four-color process and the book is printed by offset.